Cars Coloring Book

Coloring Book For Kids

© 2015 by Julie Little

All Rights Reserved. No part of this publication may be copied, reproduced in any format, by any means, electronic or otherwise, without prior consent from the copyright owner and publisher of this book.

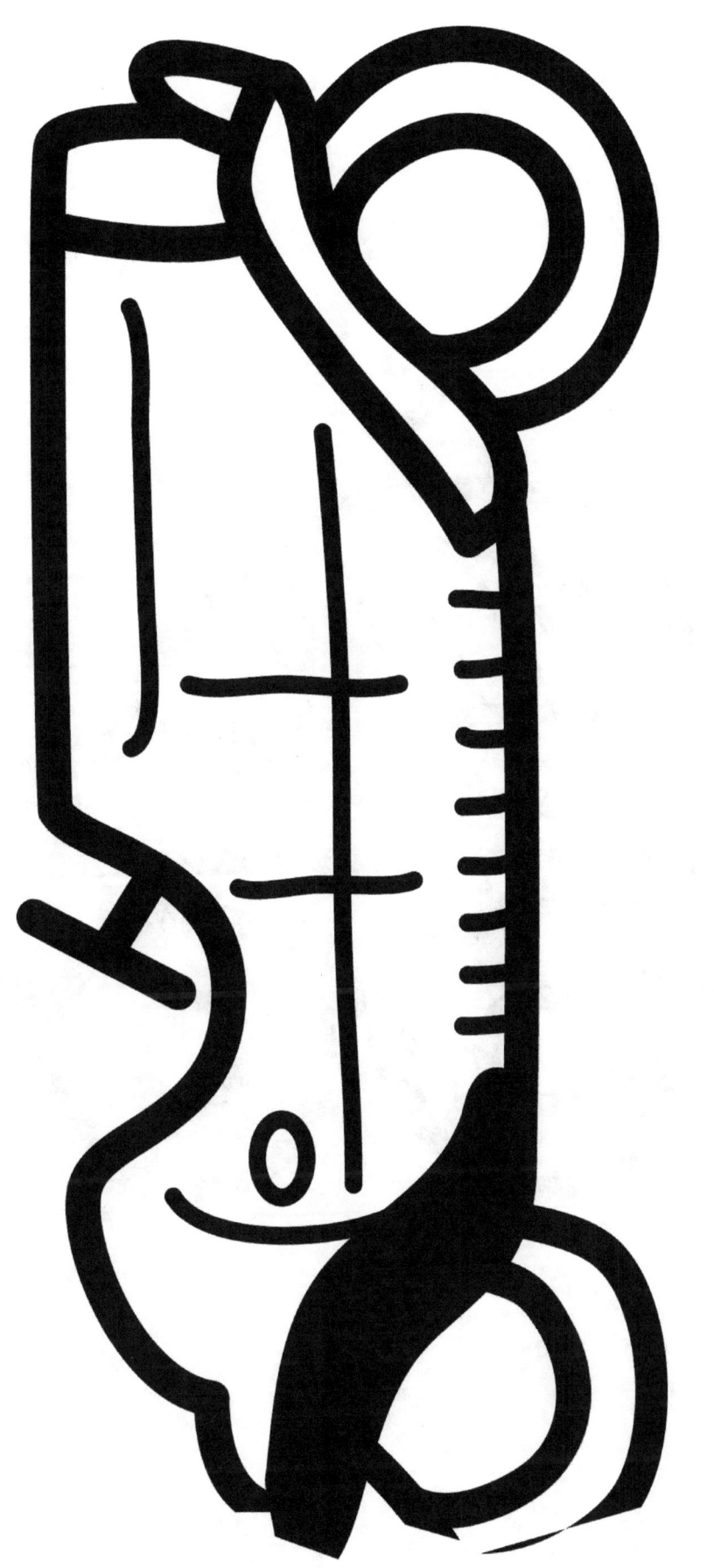

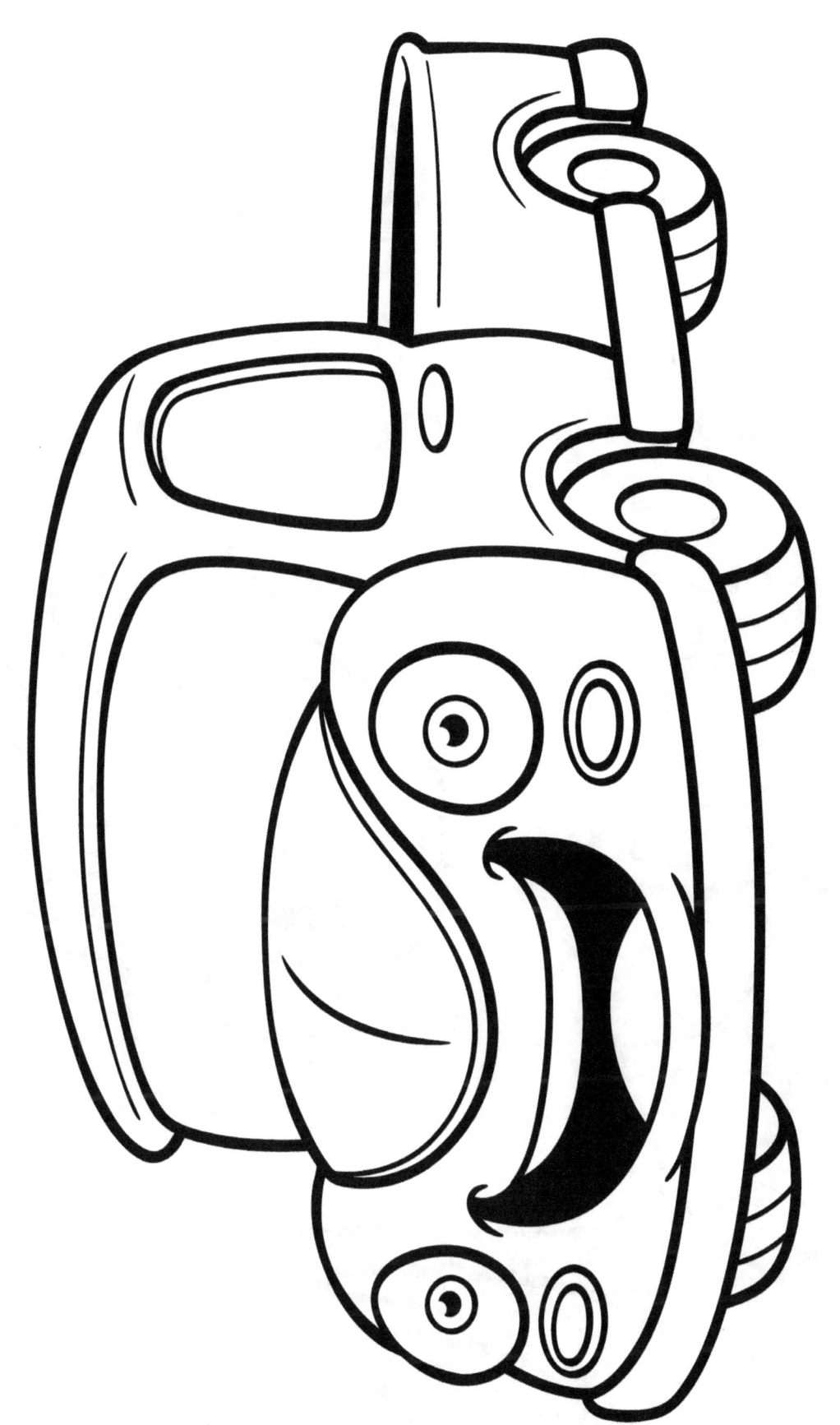

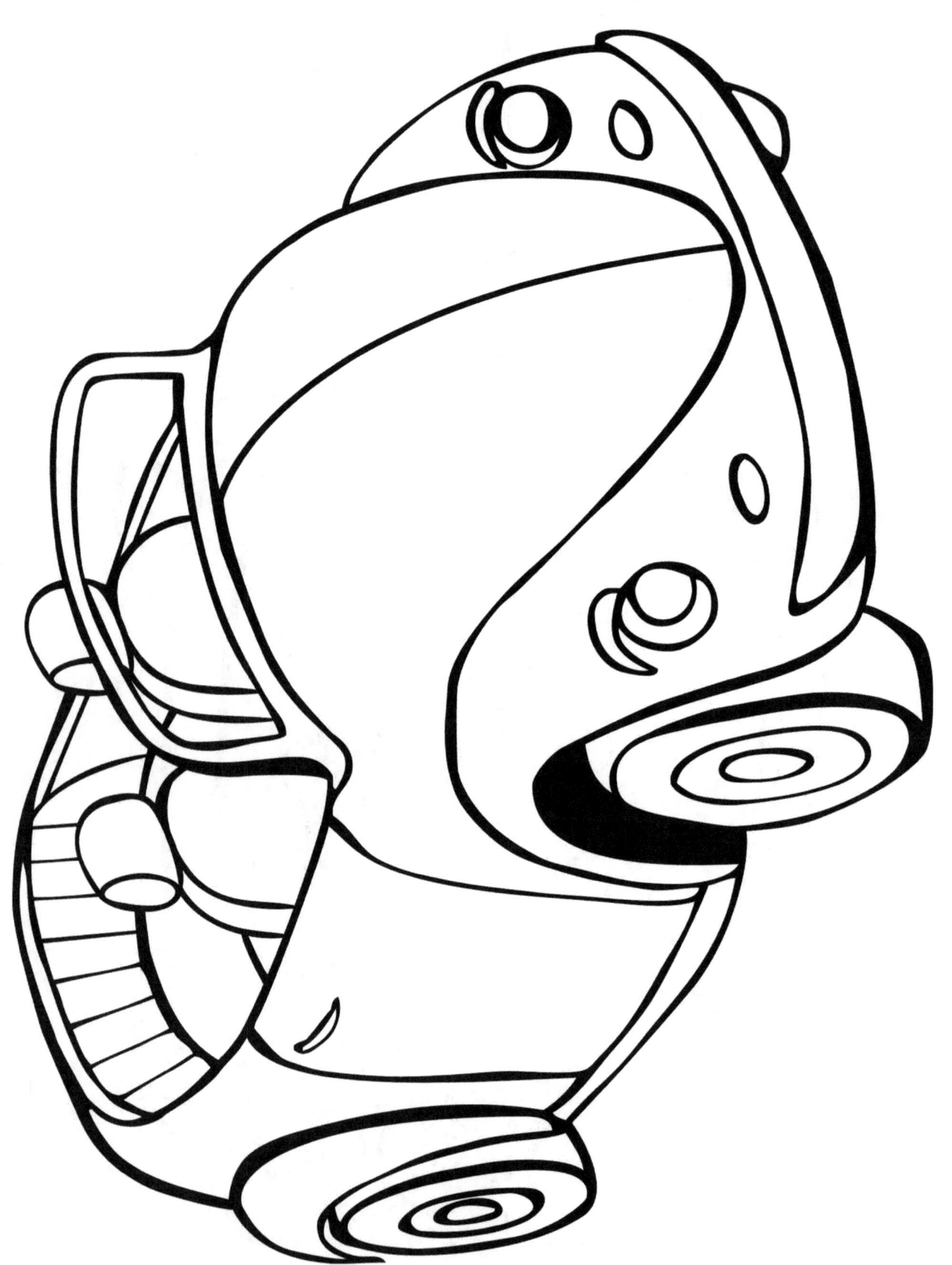

www.ingramcontent.com/pod-product-compliance
Lightning Source LLC
LaVergne TN
LVHW081548060526
838200LV00048B/2252